SIMPLE WAYS

SIMPLE WAYS

Towards the Sacred

GUNILLA NORRIS

BlueBridge

Jacket design by Amy C. King
Cover photography by Getty Images
Text design by Jennifer Ann Daddio

Library of Congress Cataloging-in-Publication Data

Norris, Gunilla Brodde, 1939-
Simple ways : towards the sacred / Gunilla Norris.
p. cm.
ISBN 978-1-933346-11-3
1. Spiritual life. 2. Meditations. 3. Devotional calendars. I. Title.

BL624.N675 2008
204'.4—dc22
2007041415

Published by
BLUEBRIDGE
An imprint of
United Tribes Media Inc.
240 West 35th Street, Suite 500
New York, NY 10001

www.bluebridgebooks.com

Printed in the United States of America

1 3 5 7 9 10 8 6 4 2

CONTENTS

Towards the Sacred
WITH OUR EVERY-DAY THINGS

Towards the Sacred
IN OUR GRATITUDE

For My Beloved Family

Why do we ask, "What is the way?"

For there are as many ways

as there are stars in the firmament.

INTRODUCTION

For many years now I have written about spirituality in the every-day. It is the *every-day* in which we live. Being human we often long for something more transcendent than the ordinary, but then we quite often miss that which is numinous and extraordinary right under our noses.

Spirit is everywhere, even in the darkest hells of human creation. As the psalmist wrote, "Where can I go from your spirit? . . . If I make my bed in Sheol, you are there." That God's Presence is everywhere is understood by many religions. We may be shaped by our cultural and familial upbringing and by specific faith traditions—but they do not ultimately define our relationship with God. It is a personal experience. We must show up for it, and we do so reliably through prayer and meditation and in the living of our daily life. If we could describe this as a relationship, a capacity to fully attend to God's Presence in the present, then we can meditate and pray anywhere and at any time.

My way has been a householder's way, opening myself as much as possible to that which is near me in order to experience God's Presence there. It is an undramatic, ordinary path, and it is completely available to anyone—even to those who do not believe in God, but who nevertheless have a faithful reverence for Life.

To pray *with*, that is, to reverently *be with*, requires a kind of dual awareness—that of the concrete, touchable world, and that which is untouchable and yet shines through the material world. We are embodied and we are spirit. So, too, are the places we dwell in and the things we use. Could we be more careful and aware of the world and our selves, we would without a doubt find that we live in a holy environment, and that the meaning of our lives can be found and experienced exactly where we are.

We have bodies, we have dwelling places, we have the things we use, and we have an inherent capacity to wonder. The poet Rainer Maria Rilke urged the young poet Kappus to try to love his questions, for then he might "gradually, without noticing live along some distant day into the answer." Could we understand prayer and meditation to be a natural condition of questioning, of openhearted wondering, which can lead us to God—the unanswerable answer? I believe this is true and have given myself to this understanding. But each of us must discover the best way for themselves.

What does it mean to wonder? It means to fully experience without mental conclusions. To wonder is open-ended and full of attention. It allows for fresh nuances, even when we seem to experience the same thing many times. To wonder is to be alive with curiosity and spaciousness and with such courtesy toward the given that it has the chance to become a gift to us. It also invites us to give ourselves back to life and so paradoxically to receive more abundantly.

There is no need to read this book sequentially. Whatever

the reader finds here that feels right could be a place to wonder, to experience, and to deepen. It can be thought of as a railing of sorts, such as staircases have. Contemplative traditions of the past created rules to live by. The medieval meaning of the word rule was *railing*—something to hang on to in the ups and downs of life. I hope these contemplative ideas could be such railings for the reader. But we know we can't get anywhere if we continually change railings. There would be too many staircases and never a landing. Should one of these simple ways appeal to you, stick to it. Continue to question, to wonder, and to use it for some time. The *Considerations for the Heart* offered in this book, or ones you pose that you like better, could be practiced for a month, a year, or a lifetime. If a question you have been with for some time loses its appeal, try another and continue with it in a steady and stable manner. Just one simple question fully lived can bring us in time into that mystery which each of us can touch and be touched by, the presence of God. The key is to give our selves to it. Only in giving our time do we discover the timeless.

Prayer or meditation partners, or committed groups, can also use this book. Once a contemplative focus is decided upon, a group can enter into its practice for a few weeks and then share their experiences. This can lead to very fruitful exchange, but more importantly, it is in having the encouragement of others that we are helped to grow our constancy.

These ways appear simple on the surface. Simple, as we know, is not easy, but it is above all doable. Something small, consistent, and doable is a worthy way to wonder. In time, our open attending will become a continuous state, a deep relatedness that can be known as prayer without ceasing. Then we will not only be graced, but *know* that we participate in a wonder-full Grace beyond imagining.

Towards the Sacred

WITH OUR BODIES

TO BE EMBODIED

What does it mean to be embodied? Doesn't it mean to be given form? We have been gifted with a particular body. It is who we are in part—but not the whole story.

Form implies content. And when form and content are wedded, an intrinsic grace emerges where beauty is revealed. To mature into such beauty takes mellowing time.

Our bodies can help us and can be avenues of prayer, for God is there in us closer than our hands or our feet. Having bodies we are invited to be incarnated spirit. We can come to learn to be conscious of our bodies as holy, as homes for spirit. That awareness alone can change how we live.

Our bodies are always with us, faithful companions to the end. They tell our stories—how we treasure or do not treasure the gift of them. Through our bodies we can participate in God's world or trash and disregard it.

To be fully alive, fully embodied is a living prayer.

MEDITATION

New light.
Just under the blinds, a sliver of light.
The light declares it is a new day—
a first day—
the only day available—
none other.

Light dawns inside as well,
felt more than seen—
a new day where we, too, are new,
brand new,
just born.

The light grows and so does the wonder
of having a form,
a body, this very body.
We are made to be particular—
a somebody.

It will take a whole lifetime
to become who we are,
to become within the gift
of the body we've been given.

CONSIDERATIONS FOR THE HEART

Today, how might I more fully receive the gift of my body?

How am I to live today so as not to miss an embodied life?

How might my body be a home for spirit today?

~

TO BREATHE

When we are born, we are born into a relationship with air, with breathing. How closely the words wind, air, life, and spirit are linked in human thought. We are creatures into whom life is breathed.

A word we have for inhaling is *inspiration*. When we are fully inspired, not only are our lungs filled—our beings are also filled, with hope, with potential, with the impetuous to express possibility.

Expired, we are over and done with, stopped . . . finished.

Our life is lived within this paradox. With every inhalation we are given life. With every exhalation we must surrender that life, for another breath to be given to us. If we could fully enter the rhythm of this paradox we would live with immediacy, and be intimate with birth and death and with life itself.

MEDITATION

Unobtrusively,
softly, gently, air enters the body.

For a moment we are expanded,
somehow made more.

Then the air leaves us.
The sound of its leaving
is like the swish of a skirt,
or the distant breaking of a wave.

There is no one who can feel this for us.
Only we can feel the rich gift of it.
No one can live this moment,
or any moment, for us.
It is ours alone.

Yet we are not alone.

Every moment Life is there,
infusing us
with the radiant risk and splendor of being.

It is breathtaking.

CONSIDERATIONS FOR THE HEART

Can just this next breath be one I *receive* instead of take?

How might there be more breathing room in my life?

What would it mean to *feel* that God is breathing me?

TO SEE

We see with more than our eyes. This is a mystery. We know that even a blind person can see in that larger sense. To see with carefulness and love is a great act of faith.

So often we are too lazy or too distracted to see with care. Images come into our retinas, and our minds have already interpreted them. We do not see without our biases, our habits of life and thought.

It is a great challenge to look upon the world and be so disposed as to try to see it for itself, without the layers our needs cover it with, and without the way our judgments divide the holiness of it.

Truthfully, we cannot escape ourselves, for even in the most transparent chambers of the heart we will realize that our view is veiled. We cannot avoid this fact—but we can nevertheless bravely turn our faces towards the world and try to see it with a loving gaze.

MEDITATION

Softening our eyes,
letting them light upon people and things gently,
without hurry,
could we feel their fundamental use as innocent?

Could we try to see without interpretations,
without requirements,
letting the world in the way a baby does,
with interest and wonder?

Could we be at prayer this way?

Could we ask our eyes to be free
of our thoughts, to re-see
our surroundings, our loves, and our tasks?

Could we sense that in God
we are so essentially seen,
so constantly regarded,
that we can know this to be love?

Could we then understand that in God
we are not condemned or defined,
but forever becoming?

⌒

CONSIDERATIONS FOR THE HEART

Today, could I look at just one thing in freedom—without grasping, judging, or denying it?

Today, could I invite my gaze to be so innocent and simple that it shines like a lamp in the dark?

Today, could I ask my eyes to be the eyes of friendliness whenever I meet a stranger or encounter something I do not understand?

~

TO HEAR

We can close our eyes, but we cannot close our ears. Without ear-lids we are in a sense always open to the world, to its noise and joy, its confusion and its deep cries. Our eardrums cannot but resonate with what is around us. We thrum, whether we like it or not.

Sometimes we drown sounds with other sounds, or we shut ourselves down and refuse to acknowledge what we are hearing. Sometimes we are caught up and lifted out of ourselves because of something we heard.

When depth is measured at sea it is done by *sounding*. And like the sea our hearts have depths we are unaware of—depths we may be frightened of.

If we listened to one another with the humility of knowing that we do *not* know, then depth would be there for both speaker and hearer; there our stories, our needs and sorrows, as well as our joys would be *sounded*. It is no accident that the old-fashioned term for being well is to be sound.

By listening deeply we can discover how healing and mysterious it is to be human, to live at once in the depth and loneliness of unknowing and in the noisy bustling commerce of ordinary days.

MEDITATION

For a few moments each day,
could we listen for the silence in each sound?
Could we match that silence
with an inner stillness of our own?

Perhaps then we would hear
that which longs to be known,
to be given refuge
in simple human awareness and inclusion.

To listen to another fully
is to offer the heart like a vast sea.
That offering enlarges us.
Sometimes the heart is stirred up as surf is in a storm.
Sometimes it is becalmed and shiny with peace.
But always it is asked to be moved
by the great rhythm of meaning,
the deep and constant waves
of life requesting to be lived,
known, and heard.

CONSIDERATIONS FOR THE HEART

Next time I am listening to another, might I listen with a sense of great space, a capacity of heart as vast as the sea?

Today, can I begin to hear others without always inserting the opinions and the priorities of my little self?

Today, could I try to hear below the surface of my conversations? Could I welcome the ache and the beauty of life wanting to speak and to be heard?

TO SPEAK

We often forget that who we are speaks to others all the time, whether we open our mouths or not. From time to time our being may be silent and still, yet it emanates. It speaks without words.

For some this awareness leads to self-consciousness. They feel too exposed, too vulnerable for the usual interactions. Some babble and seek continual reflection and confirmation from others as a reassurance that they are fine and lovable.

To accept and trust that each of us is a word of God places the burden of worthiness on God, instead of on our battered, confused self-assessments.

We can turn towards God and ask to be the word God would have us be. That would mean frequent pausing to listen first before we succumb to the easy, reactive way in which we often converse.

To be spoken *through* is to be instrumental. Joy awaits us there and discovery, too, for God wants to express abundant life through us more than we imagine or recognize.

If we allow our speech to come out of intuition and silence, out of a connection with God's love, we might discover how we are re-created all the time, and how we can co-create with God.

MEDITATION

No doubt, the first human words
were grunts and growls, cries and humming.
We expressed mostly through action and signaling sounds.

What a marvel and mystery it is then
that language developed and the possibility of
expressing subtle things
far beyond guarding food and turf!

Every word we have was gained through countless years
of human use. Our lives and thoughts are shaped
by language. We live in the historical stream of it.

By expressing we explore. All over the world, in this moment,
lives are being enriched with beauty and understanding,
or destroyed—all by the use of words.

Could we honor our speaking with more reverence
by remembering this long history
and the responsibility it gives us?

Could we daily offer our speaking to God
with the knowledge that so much of our future
is created word by word?

~

CONSIDERATIONS FOR THE HEART

Today, could I learn to pause just a little moment before I speak? Might I consider whether any hasty word might limit me or someone else?

Could I consider that, whether I speak or not, I am a word of God, and therefore my dignity is inherent?

This day, could my words be gentle and my tone full as one who has been given much? Could I be well-spoken?

~

TO TOUCH

In the courtesy of beholding, and with a certain kind of respectful distance, we can come to know that everything and everyone has a vast solitude within.

Quite often we do not want to feel this essential alone-ness. It is fearful. We want to touch and be touched. We want to be verified. So we grab what we think we need and are assuaged for a brief time.

And if we do not like what comes close to us, we push it away. Confined by the ego's solid refusals, we mistake our boundaries of "not liking" for a true self. Thus experience remains on the surface, only skin-deep. We are out of touch.

To truly touch another we must relate from that inner place that never insists or resists, but only *is*. First we must bear that mystery ourselves. We must let it open us, the way a great field invites us when the gate stands ajar and we step out on ground whose furthest dimensions are and remain always unknown.

We touch with hands, with speech, and with action. That was *touching*, we say when we realize that something unnamable and sweet has happened to both giver and receiver.

Those are perhaps the moments when the gates to our inner solitudes stand ajar and something glancing passes through. Soul to soul, we are met and are touched.

MEDITATION

When our hand rests gently
on the hand of another,
when it lifts a cup,
when it opens a door,
could we feel that there are worlds beyond the seeming
boundaries beneath our fingers?

Could we, if only momentarily, sense
how much space there is in everything,
and how ecstatic with life?

Science tells us that molecules dance
in our fingers, and in all that we touch.
Could we touch with the care
of those who would fall into step
with a pattern of movement,
an ongoing dance?

Might we touch without invasion,
and yet with the joy of full participation?

CONSIDERATIONS FOR THE HEART

At least once today, could I touch without a purpose or a need?

Daily, could I caress something or someone with the awareness that I touch an inherent holiness?

Could this day be one in which I allow myself to be defenseless for a moment in the presence of another?

~

TO WALK

We both walk away from things and towards them. We speak of a person's walk of life. We admire those who walk their talk. Whether in protest or in praise, walking implies intention, direction, and purpose.

Walking has been used as a way of devotion and prayer for thousands of years. Walking on pilgrimages, circumambulating holy mountains and shrines have been faithful ways for many. Our lives are lived one step at a time. We set out on our seemingly outer journeys to arrive at something inner.

To walk we have to be upright. Just this gives us stature. To walk we have to cover ground, which means we are supported by the earth with every step. And by its nature walking creates rhythm. We learn in time to pace ourselves.

If we are conscious and embody these fundamentals when we walk, we are invited to set out with a rich awareness, a context of being to which we can contribute our wills and our efforts.

How we walk this life is our own journey. But what we come to be is the gift we are to share with others. As we walk we can know that each devoted step has its moment. As more steps follow, we may find that they have become momentous.

MEDITATION

Standing erect, feet on the ground,
could we feel how we belong—
here between heaven and earth?

As we lift a foot and place it down,
could we remember that everywhere we step
is holy ground?

When we take our steps,
our arms swinging,
and air flowing past us,
could we feel how moving
it is to have the freedom to walk?

Could we step lightly this day?
If we must hurry, could we do so slowly?
Could our walking be a continual awareness
that we journey always in God?

CONSIDERATIONS FOR THE HEART

Today, could I pick a small distance and walk it with awareness? Could I savor my body's gift of freedom to move?

Today, could I ask if the direction I am walking in my life is my choice, or merely habit?

Today, could I bless the ground I step on and appreciate its full support?

TO SLEEP

It may seem strange to some of us to think that entering into sleep could be prayer. Many of us say prayers before we turn off the light, but we seldom think of *consciously* giving ourselves over to the losing of our daytime awareness for the mysteries of sleep and dreams.

Attended, this process is a lived prayer of trust, a meditation of self-abandonment in God. Nightly we can practice the transition we must one day make into death, into the ultimate unknown.

We might lie for some time under our covers in the dark and remember the events of the day—our joys and our regrets. We might even pray about these things, but in the meantime our bodies are sinking into rest. They are taking a simple, direct route. Letting go, they are far more trusting than our minds with their constant concerns.

For us letting go and letting be is first and foremost a body prayer. At night we can learn to find ease, to be at rest in God, and so to grow to live our days without restlessness.

Who we are is impossible to define. We can only let go into a larger keeping. We may then experience the death of control and might feel a birth into that which holds the stars in their courses, the tides in their rhythm, the seasons in their turning. Our little troubles diminish in that great silence, and we learn to be at peace.

MEDITATION

Peeling off our clothes and stripping away
our daytime concerns,
could we become available to silence?

Could we turn these acts of "getting ready" for sleep
into offerings?
Could we come to our night bed
as we actually are—naked
to God?

For the short time between being awake
and being asleep, might we surrender
everything?

Could we open to the gift of rest,
that gift in which
new beginnings are embedded?

Could we accept that just here, in our sleep,
we move forward,
or rather, we are being moved forward
in the vast Love
that wants us each to fully be?

CONSIDERATIONS FOR THE HEART

Tonight, as I take off my clothes, could I take off my self-concerns and self-recriminations? Could I be simple—without concepts, naked to being as I am?

Under the cover of night could I know that light shines from distant stars and from a Love that holds both them and me in every moment?

Might I rest tonight in God? Might I let go? Might I learn to die daily and so live?

Towards the Sacred

IN OUR
DWELLINGS

DWELLING

To dwell is to live in a place, to remain in it. Any space we truly occupy becomes, through dwelling, a home—becomes, through time, a sanctuary.

There is, in the word *dwell*, a sense of repose. When we really inhabit our homes we gain a sense of time, and are then more able to know where we are, who we are, and how we might grow.

The structures we live in are full of symbols, abundant archetypes. Windows, walls, roofs, and floors—how deep are their meanings! We live with them on a practical level, but we also live with them as icons that have implications for our inner being. We live with the *spirit* of them.

To deeply sense that spirit we need to linger, we need to tarry. We need to abide and to settle. When we do, we will in time leave the ordinary way we rush, and enter the radiance of being in the eternal now where God is—and where we always actually are. It is there that we are meant to be. It is there that we live our true lives.

MEDITATION

Standing on the floor,
noticing the walls rise up
to hold the roof over our heads,
could we be aware that we are in the space
where our lives take place, where we reside?

Could we inhabit it with our spirits,
feel the spaciousness that is there,
give ourselves to it, and so receive
in return?

The structure waits for us
to make it hospitable,
to notice its possibilities
and its beauty.

It waits to reflect the truth
back to us that beauty is
in the eye of the beholder.

Such beholding is hospitality,
for in such recognition
even the poorest place becomes rich—
a human dwelling.

CONSIDERATIONS FOR THE HEART

Today, could I be grateful for the sweet shelter my home gives to me?

Today, could I linger in the spirit of place—sense it breathing with me, and know that God is everywhere here?

What of beauty could I offer to God today in my dwelling?

⁓

THE DOOR

We enter our dwellings through a door. When the door closes we are *within* the protection of our home. Yet we do not always want to be enclosed and protected. We also want to let the world in, to crack the door, to set it ajar, to invite that which is new into the trusted and familiar.

A door is often emotionally associated with the need to say both yes *and* no. We might slam a door to express a definite *no*. Then, when we unlock a door, we are in a mode of unlocking more than we know. It could be sensed as a willingness to encounter, to open and to grow, to allow and to let in.

There are a number of actual doors in our homes, and many more doors within us than we could ever be aware of. We can touch the doorknob of our front door and use that gesture to sense what should be invited into our lives, and what must be refused.

As we begin to notice doors—our own doors and those of others—we could explore where our inner doors might be jammed and need their hinges oiled. We could find out where we have been unconscious of sealed attitudes, where we groan when asked to open.

We can make one door in our home the object of inner study—to better embrace how we might appropriately open and close.

MEDITATION

Could a hand on the doorknob
remind us that we have the power
to unlock our inner doors?

Could we pause here
and feel this moment
as one of decision-making?

We may only be going into a familiar room,
but we can enter it with the understanding
that every day we enter into our habits,
our attitudes, our inner living rooms.

How might we be recalled into the present
by turning the handle of this door?
Could we use it as a means to slow down,
to ask ourselves what new doors there are to pass through,
both in our relationships
and occupations?

Could turning the handle of this door
be an opening to prayer?

CONSIDERATIONS FOR THE HEART

What knocks at my inner door? What welcome guest or unknown fear is asking to be given sanctuary this day?

When a door closes in my life, could I be thankful for what once was? Might I look for the door through which I am now asked to pass?

When I enter my home or close the door for the night, may I remember those who have no doors to keep them in safety? Could I reach out to them in some helpful way?

~

THE FLOOR

We don't seem to pay attention to the floor unless it is missing, unless it has a spill or an obstruction on it. Mostly we are confident that the floor is present and we merrily step upon it.

Many things become floor-like to us—certain steady relationships, certain habits, certain ongoing expectations. When we are *floored* by something, the unexpected has happened to us. Our usual experience is interrupted, and we *land* not on habitual ground but on the firmness of reality.

Feeling the floor with our bare feet is a good experience in mindfulness. Every morning we can step out of our beds, out of our night dreams, and stand on an actual floor. The day can be grounded by this act of attentiveness.

As we put our feet on the physical floor we can ponder what might serve as an inner floor for us to stand on that day—what intentions, what activities, what attitudes. Over time we may come to know what ground we rely on.

The simple act of connecting the mind to the feet to the floor is very steadying. In time it makes the word *understand* into something lived and vital.

MEDITATION

Each time we rise out of bed,
or out of a chair,
the floor is there to meet us.
We have a welcoming somewhere to put our feet.

Could we feel this to be spiritually true as well?
Could we more and more come to trust
that there is a Ground of Being,
and that we are asked to know
where we stand?

Could we come to appreciate
that the floor is level,
and that it also levels us?
Eternal Ground is everyone's ground.

Might the soles of our feet
become soulful,
so that we might walk on any floor
with both equanimity and equality?

CONSIDERATIONS FOR THE HEART

In the way floorboards fit tongue in groove, might I also find a place where I fit exactly and have a special opportunity to be of solid support for others?

Always the floor is there, ready to bear. Daily, may I learn to bear up when I am called to the difficult?

At least once a day, could I appreciate the floor that I stand on? Through feeling it, might I also feel that greater Ground which holds me?

~

THE WALL

Many people who meditate sit facing a wall—facing a limit in order to find the limitless inside. Many pilgrims have traveled to stand beside the Wailing Wall in Jerusalem or to be witnesses by the walls where the names of the dead are inscribed. We need walls to help us with memory and grief, as well as with the daily need for safety and support.

We know a wall will stop us. It rises above us. It shapes enclosures. The walls in our homes support the roof and create the structure of our rooms. We need them. They are a kind of second skin made of wood, of brick, of plaster or cement, of straw and mud. Their presence shapes how we can live and what will happen in a space. Our lives are led within actual walls—and within the walls of our minds.

It is hard to embrace both the inner and outer walls that limit us. These walls can be both challenging and trustworthy friends, for they gather us into specific spaces, into the present, into what is actual and true. Then and there we can begin to be accepting, to know and outgrow what no longer serves us. Only when we are against the wall—and truly know it—can we begin to deconstruct the walls that separate us from each other and from God.

MEDITATION

The walls of our homes are silent,
yet they speak.

Their height reminds us
to rise above complaint,
to give patience and space
to what confines us.

They surround us and hold us.
Within them we are protected.
They are the intimate witnesses of our lives.
They stand by us.

These walls define where we are.
They recall us to the present,
the time we have been given—
the day, the hour, the minute, the second.

We are reminded that it is within limits
that our lives are forged.

CONSIDERATIONS FOR THE HEART

There are always limits—both inner and outer walls. What limit must I accept today with equanimity?

What limits in my life might I question, might I be able to rise above?

Within the limits of my walls, how might I discover a life in God's limitless Presence?

THE STAIRCASE

Most days we use the stairs of our homes without a thought about their possible meaning beyond enabling us to climb. And often we don't even think about that obvious use. Yet stairs and ladders have always been powerful spiritual images.

Humans have forever wanted to transcend the earthly plane and ascend to the heavenly realms. Stairs lead us to the tops of pyramids and towers. Native American Kivas, dug deeply into the ground, are likewise numinous places. From a chamber within the earth a ladder ascends through an opening into light. It is a human aspiration to be grounded, of earth, and yet to ascend, to know ourselves as beings of light.

Up and down goes the way. It cannot do otherwise. Coming and going we are always in process between levels of feeling and experience, between time and timelessness. And yet we can only take one step at a time. Stairs let us see this very clearly, for each tread is measured. Whether up or down, we have to take the one step just in front of us.

Making a habit of turning to prayer when we use the staircase, we might come to experience how realms in life are not so separate. Though they are not always clear to us, they are nevertheless all there at once. With gratitude we might realize the ancient wisdom, "as above, so below."

MEDITATION

With a foot on the treads
we feel the lift of going up. There is joy
in this simple movement.

We hold on to the staircase railing,
and to our inner railing—that decision
to pay attention,
to be with just the next step.

Could we feel solidarity
with pilgrims everywhere
who have climbed up to holy shrines
or down to crypts of meaning?

Could we pray with each step we take,
so that ascending or descending
we might come to feel
that our homes are sanctuaries?

Then soon the familiar stairs—
that vertical hallway—
will become a holy way.

CONSIDERATIONS FOR THE HEART

Could I learn today that up *and* down is the way? Could I forgo asking which is better?

This day, could I not live ahead of myself but be willing to take one step at a time?

Might I remember each day that up and down are held equally in God's embrace?

~

THE ROOF

To have a roof over our heads is to have a home. Days of storm, days of intense sun, gray days, pleasant days—the roof is there and we are sheltered.

How easily we take that fact for granted, yet all around us there is homelessness—a roof-less population. In appreciating that we are protected, can we reach out and be sufficiently human to help shelter the unsheltered?

Every time we hear rain or sleet on the roof when we are inside is to know we are safe. Can we move from that physical actuality into gratitude and then into action on behalf of those who have no roof?

Under God's wings we are all sheltered, and thus we are asked to shelter one another. This may mean sharing our homes, our labor, or our money. But there are other roofs we can provide as well that are not made of matter. They are willing extensions of care, lean-tos of support that can give shelter in a storm.

MEDITATION

Realization is a process of recognizing the real.
It means repeated experiences of knowing.
It means integration of those experiences.

Thatched roofs, mud-daubed roofs,
tar paper roofs, asphalt and shingle roofs—
roofs are so ubiquitous, who even notices them?

The ones who have no roofs!

To feel the roof over our heads every day
is to realize our privilege of being sheltered.

Any sense of gratitude for such shelter
is only real if we act on it.
To step under the roof
would then become an act of thanks,
as well as a deep awareness
of the despair that homelessness
of any kind must be.

Could we find ways to be part of the answer?

CONSIDERATIONS FOR THE HEART

My roof is a blessing—a silent, sheltering presence. How intimately can I feel this blessing today?

Could I join the silent presence of the roof? Could I learn to be still enough to feel the over-vaulting grace of God?

What does it mean to be in the shelter of God's wings? Surely I am there with everyone. Then must not sharing be the only way?

THE WINDOW

If we have been out in the dark, how comforting to see a lighted window; if we have been shut in, how refreshing when the light finds us.

Without windows a house is a tomb. We need light and air. We need the new day to enter our homes, to bring us out of the night's slumber and out of our habits of inattention. Windows teach us to be transparent, to allow the flow of light both in and out.

If we became window *watchers*, we would clear ourselves daily for God to shine through us. That kind of transparency requires letting go of *our* agenda. It requires a willing openness, an unguarded presence.

How very challenging it is to be like a clear window, especially in difficult situations. We are asked not to force or to add anything extra to the events, to allow light to emerge, and to trust that it will.

When we stand by a window we might be able to feel the meeting of in and out, and how they mingle there at the see-through glass. It takes courage to be transparent like that in our interactions with others—to be seen and to see others clearly.

To be transparent as a window is to welcome the unknown, to allow the unexpected, and to find light in all that is familiar.

MEDITATION

The blind rolls up. Light enters
and shows us where we are.
Windows allow for no fooling.

What would it mean to realize
that every one of us is a window
where life shines through?

Could we stand to know
how every moment reveals this?
Anyone paying attention could see if we were open
or shut, spattered or clear!
A blind could not hide us—
we would only be revealed as covered.
No one would be fooled.

Could we trust that it is safe to be
without subterfuge?
Then we would be clear enough
for light to come through us naturally.

~

CONSIDERATIONS FOR THE HEART

Today, even for a very short moment, could I practice transparency—a willingness to be present without an agenda?

Could I notice every day how light finds me through a window, through certain events? Could I let it find me?

What can I see clearly now that I haven't been able to see before? Can I clean my inner window?

THE HEARTH

Not many homes have an actual hearth, a place for fire to burn freely. Most of us live in apartments or houses without fireplaces. Nevertheless, every dwelling has a subjective center for fire. It is the place where we gather, the place we are warmed.

It is no accident that the word *heart* is central to the word *hearth*. If we reflect for a moment about the heart of our home, we will have a sense of it straight away—whether it is lit with wood and matches or not, it is still the hearth place.

We may know it as an actual physical space, but it is far more. It gathers and holds us. To be brought to the fire to be warmed is an ancient form of hospitality. Every time we come together we are enacting it. At the end of the day, at festivities, at moments of grief, at all the occasions for being joined or deeply alone we are by the hearth. Here we are brought more deeply into dwelling. And it is here that our hearts are kindled.

MEDITATION

Our homes are enclosures that breathe.
Dwelling in them we bring our spirit
to the spirit of the place.

Could we daily be aware that
much like wood is brought to a fire,
we must bring ourselves to our homes
for them to be vibrant and alive?

Over time an atmosphere builds,
a sensible spirit unfolds.
It greets those that visit our homes,
and it greets us when we have been away.

When love of ourselves
and love for others
are wedded to love of place,
then a bright fire burns in the hearth
and we are deeply warmed.

~

CONSIDERATIONS FOR THE HEART

Could I notice today if the spirit of place is alive and well? If not, where have I been neglectful?

In what deepening ways can I bring more to the hearth?

When I am centered in God, my hearth will be centered as well. Could I allow God to build a new fire in my heart?

⌒

Towards the Sacred

WITH OUR
EVERY-DAY
THINGS

CARE OF THINGS

The things we use daily serve our needs, and we in turn must take care of them. When such care is not haphazard, not just getting through chores, but becomes a way to pay attention, we may find we live with things that grow to be luminous for us. From daily use they become full of association, memory, and presence.

In our throwaway culture to pray with a few every-day things might be revolutionary. It could lead us to taking more care not only of what we have, but also of that which is all around us.

There are a limited number of things we can be personal with—and most of us have too much. This understanding can bring us to pare down to what we really need, and to let go of that which we cannot hold in caring awareness. We may learn that having too much can be another form of poverty.

There are prayers all around us. They are close at hand. We can select a few objects to help us remember ourselves into the presence of the holy, and allow them to become companions on the way.

MEDITATION

When we use things in a throwaway manner,
we, too, are somehow thrown away.
We invite disregard.

For convenience and speed we let go of
living moments that are our precious life.
We hurry towards a deadline
instead of savoring a lifeline.

Could we enjoy a cup and really drink from it?
Could we peacefully clear our tables and our minds?
Could we linger with ordinary objects
and discover the prayer in them?

Objects in themselves have integrity.
We seem to think so when we send them in the mail—
Handle with Care, our packages say.

Could we learn to do so daily
during the little distances that things are handled
and moved from here to there?
Could we move with care,
touch with care, and ever so slowly become
care-full?

CONSIDERATIONS FOR THE HEART

What things have more than transitory meaning for me? Could I take better care of them and so better receive what I have?

What delights me with its presence? Could I come to feel that God delights in me also?

What in my care can be given away? What can be gained by letting it go?

A STONE

We pick up shells and stones on the beach because something about them is pleasing. We leave them on our shelves and windowsills to touch now and then and to enjoy again. But to make something a real presence in our lives we must use it often and get to know it intimately.

Many people have used rosary beads, mala beads, ankhs and crosses, amulets and crystals, as objects of significance. If we are not drawn to a specifically religious object, perhaps a little, ordinary stone will do.

To hold one thing prayerfully for a space of time day after day is deeply anchoring. It reminds us to hold on to the one, central thing—our relationship to God. It can remind us that we are, and have always been held, by God's Presence. We do not need to beg or bargain for that gift. We only need to be reminded of it often.

A little stone can provide such reminding. Worked with, it can be a cornerstone for our prayer practice. In time a real foundation might begin with it.

MEDITATION

A little stone grows warm in our hands.
The moisture from our skin makes it glisten,
just as any loving touch makes what is touched
glisten with life.

We hold it in prayer like an anchor,
to keep our thoughts from drifting away.
So small and seemingly insignificant,
it marks each day with its little weight.

"Be here with God," it tells us.
"As you hold me, you are held,
enveloped by God's constancy."

For just this moment,
could we let go of everything?
Could we boldly accept God's love
and be warmed by it, moistened into life?

Could we allow a little stone to be
a cornerstone in the house of being?

CONSIDERATIONS FOR THE HEART

To do something small and simple in constancy is to practice willingness—a wordless prayer. Could I hold a little stone, for a little while, each day and just *be willing*?

What will I stick to and with in my life? What do I actually give devotion to?

Could a little stone be in my pocket all day? Could my hand around it bring me into the hands of God?

A BOWL

An empty bowl is a wonderful symbol of openness. It will teach us to be receptive, to allow our hearts and spirits to align with God's desire for us. Using a bowl or a cup as a prayer object can, over time, help us recognize that we ourselves are vessels for God.

When our inner bowl is full to overflowing we are asked to trust that we can be response-able to hold what we must. We will also accept that our limits are not bad, but exact.

Sometimes our inner bowl—like the outer one—will just feel empty and useless. But more often, in the act of holding our bowl, we will find that we are simply at rest, in quiet, and at peace. We become filled because we are empty of all but that willingness to be present to God. We receive what is given, and it is more than enough.

Seeing our empty bowl day in and day out, holding it in our hands again and again, bringing it close to our chest, we may develop that inner quality of openness that is known as simplicity of heart. We learn to want only what we have, and to see what we have in fresh new ways.

Over time we may experience that God trusts us and has confidence in us. Then our planning and fretting will often diminish. A steady quiet will begin to settle us. Receiving daily without preconceptions, we become receptacles of grace.

MEDITATION

When a bowl rests in our hands
we feel the rim with our fingers—
the inner walls, the sturdy foot.
It holds what it can—
teaching us to hold what we can, and no more.

Against our chest this object feels hard
and stubbornly truthful. Without question
it shows us we must empty out in order to receive—
for in that emptiness is our usefulness
and our fulfillment.

How radical and fierce it feels
to start out continually empty!

Making a holy space for grace
is an every-day task.
We cannot live a dynamic faith
with day-old receiving.

Sometimes full to bursting,
sometimes empty for days,
how do we ever know what gift is there for us,
unless we are empty enough to receive it?

CONSIDERATIONS FOR THE HEART

A bowl demonstrates limits. It can only hold what it can hold. What am I unrealistically holding?

What am I refusing to fully hold even though it is mine to do?

Can I be open enough to neither expect, deny, nor judge how life fills my bowl?

A CANDLE

Candlelight has all the associations of the past when, with a fire, it was the only source of light. Lighting a candle is different than lighting an electric lamp. A candle is a living, flickering light. It can easily be blown out.

As we watch a candle burn we see the wax diminish. It melts away—a symbol for life. We each have light to give, and in the giving we use ourselves up.

Candles have long been central to worship. By lighting them we announce that we are entering into a different sense of time. Not the usual ticktock time of daily living, but sacred time, a timeless time.

When we light candles on our dining room tables we signal a time for family or friendship—a time for being together.

A lit candle cannot be left to burn by itself safely. We have to be there to tend it. How apt then it is to light a candle to begin a prayerful time.

MEDITATION

As we strike the match there is a small rasping sound.
A flame appears.
With it our candles can begin to burn.

This small act is a deep ritual—a decision
to leave our outward concerns
and turn inward to the Source of all light.

We do this in solidarity with all those who
are lighting candles to begin their prayers.
We are a multitude.

The candle flame encourages us
to stop and be present where we are.
It reminds us of our own inner flames that leap and dance
around the wick of our attention.

The wax melts. It shows us how we must give ourselves entirely
to find ourselves.

There is an inner longing that asks this of us,
for only so will it become be-longing.

In melting do we not become God's lights?

CONSIDERATIONS FOR THE HEART

How might I be alight today with warmth and possibility?

When my flame feels as if it is blown out, can I learn to trust, to wait in patience for it to be rekindled?

Can I know each day that whatever light I have is only mine to give away?

A SHAWL

In many spiritual traditions people have covered their heads in prayer. Medieval monks had hooded robes. To be under the hood helped them to turn inward, to have custody of their eyes and ears. It encouraged them to keep their curiosity in check, to not wonder about another's way and so be distracted from their own.

To not compare ourselves with others, to not envy or judge, or even to be curious, brings the mind back home to our own interiority. When the head is covered it may also tell others we are not to be disturbed.

A simple act to initiate prayer is to wrap ourselves in a shawl. The body and the mind are then signaled to center, to focus inward. We are consenting to be clothed in God-awareness.

Over time a prayer garment becomes a habit in both senses of the word. Slowly, daily, we are wrapped into silence and so into the rapture we were made for.

MEDITATION

A shawl can cover our shoulders and our heads.
Soft and familiar, it holds us
like a blessing. In it we know where we are.

Within its quiet embrace we can silence
our chattering minds. We can let go
of our curiosity about others—
and even the curiosity about ourselves.

Cocooned we are more willing to just be
in unknowing.
Though it is happening to us,
what we become is ultimately God's doing,
not ours. We can rest
in the midst of transformation,
and even in dissolution.

If we are to grow wings
they will appear in due time.
And in the meantime,
is it not enough to know that we are
clothed each day in blessing?

~

CONSIDERATIONS FOR THE HEART

I put on clothes every day, and whether I am aware of it or not, I also put on attitudes. What will I be wearing today?

How does my day change when I let myself be wrapped up in blessing?

Shawls can be sat upon. They can be spread out like table-cloths. They can carry babies and groceries. Might I let a shawl carry me into prayer?

A CLOTHESPIN

So many things can be prayer objects for us—little icons that we may use to recognize a deeper reality. One such simple household object is the clothespin. Two pieces of wood and a spring become a means to hold something fast.

If we looked a little deeper we would recognize how we, too, are often like these pieces of wood. We want solitude, for instance, and yet we have more obligations than we can meet. We are angry about something, and yet we want to be forgiving. Again and again we face these basic conflicts. We tend to bounce from one pole to the other to avoid the center—the steel spring where the discomfort coils tightly around itself.

To be willing to accept a dynamic tension builds spiritual muscle and is a challenging form of prayer. Holding two truths in balance—even seemingly opposite truths—a third tends to emerge in time . . . something we never could have imagined or known that we wanted.

We have to try this to experience it. We might begin by clarifying the opposites we are trying to bring to resolution. We can learn to trust that there is, somewhere, a hidden balance for these tensions—a releasing solution, a living answer.

MEDITATION

A clothespin rests in our hands.
We know there are many more in the basket.
Could we stick to just one issue at a time?

When we have taken the time to face
and understand an issue we are dealing with,
we have begun to be free.
We have a real chance then
to take up the task of resolution
with a willing attitude.

This willingness is a way
to not suffer our suffering, but to allow
two opposites to be held near one another
without diminishment of either.

We need rest—
and yet we must continue what we are doing.
We are confused—
and yet we must act with clarity.
We are deeply committed to something—
and yet we long to act as if we were without constraint.

It is good to write a conflict down,
as a dynamic, positive question,
and as a chosen prayer.

The clothespin will hold the piece of paper.
Placed where we can see our words often,
we will be encouraged to trust the tension
and so to live into a God-given answer.

CONSIDERATIONS FOR THE HEART

Today, could I learn to be a little less afraid of my inner conflicts? Could I move towards just one and embrace it?

Could I be in less of a hurry for easy resolutions? Could I trust God's timing?

Could I know that complaint and avoidance is not true suffering, only the suffering of my suffering? It leads nowhere. Could I instead be as simple and patient as the clothespin in holding what I must?

A JOURNAL

We hear the holy in different languages and through different means, but God speaks to us all.

One possible way to hear is by keeping a journal. When we sit, pen in hand, before the blank page waiting, we are asking our mind to also be blank. We are asking our hand to write down not so much what concerns us, but rather those intimations we sense from the *still, small voice.*

We hear this voice when we stop insisting on being the center of attention. We hear it when our hearts want the truth, when we are patient, when we have no agenda.

To give words to the often mute and mysterious movement of God within us is like giving voice to a wave. We must flow with it, sink and rise with it, and merge with the living water.

It may be as we sit with our journal that only a few words are spelled out for us now and then. But if we truly experience those words they will soak us in meaning. Day by day to wait and to listen with an open journal in our hands, and with hearts as open as the book, we will learn to hear God in our own language.

MEDITATION

The blank page invites us to be present.
A hand rests on the paper.
We know that nothing might come of this today,
but we hold the pen in an expectancy
without intention.

Even as we brood over the page,
could we feel God brooding over us?
Something is maturing in us.
New life is coming to be.

Silence gathers in the tip of the pen.
Here, just here, at this very point
our waiting is concentrated.

Blood flows from the heart
through our arms and out to the fingers,
to this little point
where the ink emerges.

The words that come may be awkward,
but in this way they are real,
for they have been realized in the heart.

CONSIDERATIONS FOR THE HEART

My journal is my personal witness. With what attitude do I keep books on myself?

Am I aware that what I am writing is a letter to my soul?

Each day can I live the words that I receive deeply and so become a word of God?

A TABLE

A table can be so many things—from a desk to an altar. It is around the table that we gather for meals. At the table we study, play games, sort the mail, pay bills, and do so much of what is needed for a household.

Tables are often cluttered. In a rush we pile them high, be they counters, bureaus, sideboards, desks, or ordinary tables. An empty surface invites this kind of use.

Were we to clear one surface in our homes and try to keep it free of everything, we would soon find how hard that is—and how much our minds are likewise surfaces that clutter up.

Keeping a clear table is a form of hospitality, for a conscious empty space reminds us to clear ourselves and so invite our souls. Spaciousness is the home of the soul.

Even one small surface kept clear is a powerful reminder. Resting our eyes on such a cleared surface invites God's company and feeds our souls.

MEDITATION

Dust rag in hand we wipe the table.
We clear it of things—
our keys, our books and papers,
our unfinished, unsorted business.

Underneath the piles, the wood emerges,
and we are able to see the grain again.
The table reminds us to live with the grain
instead of against it.
The open surface dares us to clear ourselves, too.

Inner spaciousness requires attention,
requires a willingness to be space-keepers,
making room for God.

"The table is ready," we say at mealtimes
and invite our friends and family to partake.
If we ready a table by clearing it
we also ready our hearts.

Such a small, yet simple task is profound.
Through it we might learn to be
always ready for the holy Guest.

~

CONSIDERATIONS FOR THE HEART

How does my clutter keep me on the surface of things? What do I not want to know, to feel?

Could I daily clear one chosen surface of dust and things and know that I am clearing a sacred space inside me?

Could I take pleasure in knowing that, much like prayer flags, the cleared table is there all day—a constant prayer?

~

Towards the Sacred

IN OUR
GRATITUDE

RECEIVING

The world, our lives, our daily bread, our loved ones, our opportunities, our challenges and difficulties—all are gifts. Even the innate capacity to receive is a gift.

There is not a single moment in life in which we are not given something. We can begin to notice this; we can increase our capacity to receive daily, both that which seems small and that which is big.

If we imagined ourselves as open cisterns, we would soon become aware that we are continually being filled. Every moment we have more than enough—if we are open to receive.

It is gratitude that increases our capacity. We know the saying, "to them that have, more shall be given." The more we are aware that we have been given, the more we are given. The abundance is never ending.

What a joyous task then lies before us each day. Showered with blessings, it will take our entire lifetime to learn to be nothing but a living thankfulness.

MEDITATION

All through the day,
we can stop
just for a moment to remember
that the moment we are living is a gift to us.
Have we received it fully?

All the raw materials that provide
for life have been given to us all.
Everything we touch and see
is on loan for our common use.

Nothing is fundamentally our own,
and yet all is ours to receive.
What a paradox it is
that when we truly receive,
we are immediately stripped
of any rights of ownership.
Yet we are also, every moment, made
heirs to the world.

Fully experienced, it is an overwhelming paradox.
Can we live this strange and awesome duality
for even just one moment a day?

What small, single thing can I receive today and not take for granted?

Having received, can I let go of *possessing* what I have been given? Can I learn to have and not grab?

In which ways do I most naturally express gratitude? Could I see these ways as being gifts as well—knowing that nothing is my own, and yet I have it all?

RECEIVING NATURE

Under every stone and in every stump we can find burgeon-
ing life. Tiny life swims in a thimble full of water. With eyes
that can see, there is unstoppable life in every nook and
cranny.

God's joy is expressed in such variety that not even one
snowflake will be exactly like another. Exultation is at the
core of creation. All creation is God's self-expression and
pours forth in majesty.

Our true nature is part of this joy. And the nature we see
all around us is *expressed* joy. From fish that never see light
at the bottom of the ocean, to the lark flying so high it dis-
appears in a cloud—majesty is the home we are set in. What
can we do but copy the psalmist and sing, "Make a joyful
noise unto the Lord?"

Opened to such wonder we are shattered by the sheer
beauty of it. We can feel how we are part of the weltering
permission that is God's creation. We are insignificant in
one way and yet so infinitely precious and holy in another.
Perhaps it is only in our gratitude that we can fully feel and
understand that we are all of it.

How natural then to spend our lives in more and more
praise.

MEDITATION

On a clear night we can see the sky
through the window—
stars too staggeringly numerous to count,
and space so vast it cannot be fathomed.

As morning dawns we hear birds and insects.
They are praising the new day.
We smell mown grass and honeysuckle.
Leaves stir in the wind,
whispering about joy.

All around us is majesty.
There is even majesty in the crabgrass
growing in the flowerbeds.
All is imbued with abundant life force.

Each morning we are given a world
to be in, to enjoy, to be opened by
and grounded in.

Can we ever truly receive this gift?
How much joy can the heart hold?

CONSIDERATIONS FOR THE HEART

Today can I perceive that everything around me is part of God's glory? Can I learn not to diminish anything?

Every day, could I find something to smile about, to be tickled by? Could an appreciation of simple joys be so constant that it becomes my natural habit?

Could I learn not to shut down when my heart feels full to overflowing? Could I let myself dissolve into praise?

RECEIVING OUR
DAILY BREAD

In a day we may say thank you ten to twenty times as easily as we say hello or goodbye. But to truly receive and give thanks for our daily bread we must give more than words; we must recognize how many are the givers.

Countless hands have been at work for us to have what is on our plates. In a simple sandwich lies the farmer's toil, the miller's craft, the packager's care, the trucker's long drive, the delivery man's round, the sweat of the grocery stock boy, the checkout girl's weariness, not to speak of the cook's efforts.

Our clothing, our household goods, our cars, the services necessary for daily living are all based on people giving their time, their *life-time*. We, too, are part of this great exchange—giving to have, receiving to give. Every day we give our lives away and receive the lives of others. This is no small exchange. Can we be aware of this and be grateful?

Such gratitude will multiply our sense of interconnectedness. We will stop taking things for granted and begin to give thanks instead, noticing more and more how much we are continually being gifted. Our daily bread becomes the occasion for humility. We will realize how much our lives are dependent on others and how much each day is based on receiving.

MEDITATION

Our plates are full.
The food smells good
and steams with invitation.

Before swallowing it down,
could we stop long enough for gratitude?
Could we receive this meal
instead of gobbling it?

Every mouthful has someone's time
imbedded in it.
Could we eat with a growing awareness
of all those who have had a part
in providing us with sustenance?

This meal can become more filling
than we would ever have dreamed.
We can taste the grace.

It is as blessed to receive as to give.

⌒

CONSIDERATIONS FOR THE HEART

How much that I ingest am I truly aware of? Could I do one deliberate thing when I eat—taste in gratitude?

When I eat could I remember those who have no food? Could I give of my substance to them?

If I were really aware of the work of others in creating my food, would I need less on my plate?

~

RECEIVING OUR
RELATIONSHIPS

We are often not aware how full of expectations our relationships are—that we *should* be considered, understood, and done right by. Unstated rules, for the conduct of ourselves or another, lie like land mines on the path of our connections. The conditioned sense of one's rights, or lack of rights, ignores the holy sanctity that is at the core of each person.

To receive another at any depth, we must first receive ourselves in depth. If we really accept that from birth our being is holy and precious, we will learn to have reverence for our lives. Then it follows more naturally that we can have reverence for the lives of others. It will take a whole lifetime to discover what this might mean in expressed concern and action. But it is from such a solid base of receiving that compassion and care can flow.

Our true nature has resilience and openness. It is full of curiosity and spaciousness. God's love for us pours into our essence every moment, no matter what is going on. If we learn to lean into that deeper reality we will not have so much need to be defensive. We can rest our defense in God's presence in us, and not in our own learned reaction. We can give up the need to fight, to flee or to freeze, and begin to trust that under the surface there is always vibrant and possible life.

MEDITATION

Again and again
our usual reactivity surfaces
when someone slights us, deliberately or accidentally.
We want to defend ourselves, or more accurately,
we want to defend who we think we are—
an image usually composed of idealized pictures of ourselves,
or the dark, entrenched habits of self-deprecation.

Is this the self we really want to defend?
Could we learn to go inside instead?
Could we embrace the holy mystery of God's love for us,
and not let ourselves be defined by
either our own conditioned thoughts
or the words and actions of others?

Could we receive again our God-given self?
Could we remember that we are precious,
even though we don't fully understand it?
Could we realize that the one who is hurting us
has forgotten their preciousness, too?

Are we not already one, already whole, already trusted?
Could we begin to live out of God's trust in us?

CONSIDERATIONS FOR THE HEART

Today, could I experience that I am able to love because I am beloved?

Could I catch my defensiveness as it happens and learn to give it less power? Could I remember in mid-reaction to ask—if this is the me I want to defend?

Could I spend fruitful days looking for the holy in all those I love, but also in those who give me difficulty?

~

RECEIVING OUR
DAILY ROUND

If we count up the hours we make beds, wash dishes, run the vacuum or the lawn mower, pay bills, shop for groceries and cook, we will realize that we have spent not just days, but months and years in these activities. Every day we have a choice to just get through our daily round, or to live and savor the gift of it. This choice, however, takes deep awareness.

When we've been away either traveling or in the hospital, most of us realize that coming home feels precious. We are happy to be back with our routines, their familiarity, and at first, at least, we take them up as if reuniting with dear old friends. It is a great relief to have a daily rhythm and daily tasks.

When we truly focus on one thing we "must do" we can decide to let the task center us and give us dignity. Instead of complaining, why not be glad that we are able to do it at all? As inescapable tasks become more and more occasions for gratitude, we will know there is no place and no task where God is not—and neither is there any one activity more worthy than another.

God is always present in the smallest of details. It matters how we do the humble things of daily living. They can be occasions of burden or of praise. With awareness we can choose which it will be for us.

MEDITATION

Water runs into the sink.
The soap foams up.
Here are the dishes for the third time today!
Can we be glad of having dishes to wash—
of having water and plates?

Can starting the lawn mower
be a time to be grateful?
Can the smell of cut grass remind us
of the joys of a space well maintained?

Paying bills, washing clothes, driving children,
picking up groceries—each day is so very full
of tasks. Could we honor the gift of them
by not making them burdens?

Could we learn to take our time with them
and so find God's Presence
imbedded in each one?
Then slowly the work of our hands
and the meditations of our hearts
would come together
and be one.

CONSIDERATIONS FOR THE HEART

Today, when I grumble about having to do something, could I stop for a moment? Right there, in mid-task, could I choose to turn the doing into one of being in thanks and praise?

Could I select one task to be my special prayer and fully do it for God?

Today, could I notice how I select one thing to be more important than another? Could I learn to value even small, uninspired activities and see them as ways to be faithful?

⌒

RECEIVING OUR CHALLENGES

Trusting God with all of our life means also to be able to trust the difficulties that come our way. Challenges and bitter sufferings can be gifts as well. To open to them is a profound act of humility. When the door slams and our hopes are dashed, when our health fails, a loved one dies, when the world closes in and the air we breathe is full of despair, it is hard to receive such experiences as gift.

Years after a dreadful difficulty or loss, many people will say that it was the difficulty that was somehow a profound turning point, a gift in disguise. But in the middle of the suffering we simply want it "not to be." To pray for endurance, reprieve, help of any kind, is only natural then. But when the challenge is the kind that will not go away, we have no choice but to be in it, and with it, and to learn whatever we must learn through it.

To let go when we must is not always easy. We want things to be the way they were. To pray for our resistance to pain and loss is a big prayer. It shows that we are willing to try to accept the suffering that has come to us.

Such suffering shatters our sense of self, breaks our hearts, and lets God in. Our resistance is transformed into communion with the suffering of others. We will then belong to something eternal—God's suffering in us and with us. Even as we are broken, we also break through.

MEDITATION

We are not abandoned and alone
in suffering as much as we insist.
Could we sense that many others are suffering
the very same thing we are enduring?
Could we suffer with them and for them?

Could we sense that God suffers with us, too?
We do not need to explain or fully understand
how love is right here with us in the pain.
We only need to feel it.

How can there be hope in hopelessness?
How is despair held
in an unconceivable "nevertheless"?

We don't know. We don't know.
But unknowing is the most intimate we can be.
It is here that we can come to feel
the vast, ongoing aloneness of God.

Are we weeping God's tears
as well as our own?
Is God weeping through us?
Can we be trusted with this pain?

CONSIDERATIONS FOR THE HEART

Could I allow God's love to penetrate my outrage and suffering?

Could a perception grow within me that I do not suffer this day's sorrows alone—that many others accompany me?

Could I grow to be equal to the trust God has in me? Could I accept all of God's gifts, even the dreadful ones?

RECEIVING OUR OPPORTUNITIES

We have preconceived ideas of what we consider opportunities. Unless an opening comes in a recognizable way, we might miss it or be afraid to take a chance. So much keeps us unduly cautious—like fear of failure or a sense of our ineptitude. Lack of imagination or the inability to recognize possibility may block us away from numerous opportunities for growth and new experiences, and we continue to be locked into the same old, same old.

Our ignorance and fear are so strong because we have a deep-seated need to control. We would rather suffer the devil we know than get changed by that which is foreign and new. Opportunities are angels—moments of illumination appearing in the here and now with fresh life. These luminous moments are met with caution and hesitancy. It is hard for us to embrace them.

We won't be in control. Life will be in charge, and we will be asked to open wide and receive what comes. Our old selves will inevitably be changed, and perhaps our comfortable sense of who we are and what life is will be stretched out of recognition. Locked in our small, self-defined worlds we forget that God is always present, and that in God's presence is the infinite power of possibility. To live in that awareness and with willingness before such dynamic insistence requires flexibility. It requires us to let go. It requires a strong inner *Yes*.

MEDITATION

What if we set out every morning with curiosity,
with the intention to notice
as many opportunities as possible?
Would it not be like reading the world
as a holy book—a Lectio Divina of sorts,
that ancient practice of spiritual reading?
Every day we could be poring over
the unfolding of new and possible worlds.

There are innumerable, small opportunities
to be helpful, attentive, or kind.
Taking up these opportunities,
would we not come to know that we are
a living part of the infinite story?

But there are also countless opportunities to refrain
from harmful action: reactive annoyance, overdoing,
rushing, compulsive habits, spacing out,
and other myriad ways of not being present.
Could we slowly learn to live
the "no" that is really a deeper "yes"?

And when excitement and fear are equally mingled,
could we realize that here and now something is present
that we must consider with all our being?

Could we feel that our very own angel has arrived
at the doorstep? Could we open
and ask what love would encourage us to do?

⌒

CONSIDERATIONS FOR THE HEART

Today, could I notice the open curiosity that God has placed within me—that innocence and capacity to participate in opportunity?

Could I also understand that opportunities lie in refusing to participate in destructive habits? Then saying no will be saying yes to a greater good.

I know I cannot move mountains. Could I just take the next, possible step towards unfolding—and know that is enough?

⌒

RECEIVING THE GIFT
OF OUR BEING

The mind divides, categorizes, analyses, and defines. Our souls open, wonder, suffer, and love. To receive the gift of being we must let go of the ways we define and give names to who we are. We cannot receive the gift of our being unless we suspend our own self-conceptions and definitions. Instead, we must become soul-wise and let the love of God reveal our inner beauty and our capacities. It means consenting to God's love.

If we suspend our judging minds, we will see that what God has made is *very good*. Creation is wondrous. It is not for us to deny such gifts. The only natural response is gratitude and care.

To wake every morning knowing that we, no matter what, are fundamentally *very good* and that our neighbor is very good as well, is to wake into any new day as if it were the dawn of creation, the very first day. Receiving the inherent goodness of God's creation is the day's invitation. It happens each and every morning.

When we daily attend to this invitation with a responding intention to find goodness in our own being and the being of others, our lives will be sanctified. We come to realize that each one of us is created deeply blessed, and that we are asked to further that blessing in the way we live.

MEDITATION

So often the habit of self-criticism
creeps into our minds.
It is an almost imperceptible fog
of dislike or niggling self-correction.
Before long this judgment mists over
the gift and wonder of being,
and spills out into criticism
of others and of the world.

We may be surprised by how thickly
this fog can cover our lives.
Socked in, we are made blind.

We have stopped receiving.
We have forgotten how awesome it is to feel
our hearts pumping. They do so for decades.
Just like our cells renew themselves continuously.
Every seven years we have completely new bodies.
We can breathe, see, hear, and touch,
think, move, dance, and run.
All this we are given
without effort on our part,
without payment.

Could we come out of our fog
into the blazing light and delight
of being here at all?
Could we be awe-struck by the love
that made us,
by the sheer radiance offered us
in the gift of being?

CONSIDERATIONS FOR THE HEART

Today, could I trade proving my worth for the joy of just being?

Today, before speaking or acting, could I sense that I am infused with and surrounded by blessing?

Could grateful praise be my task today?

CLOSING

God is a word we use, and we think we know what it means. But, in truth, God is always far beyond our understanding. We can only know God by unknowing. We can only offer our willingness and our wonder. This kind of constant and open inquiry is an intense intimacy through which we take God into our being.

The simple ways described in this book are some means to remain constant, to have a rule. Whether in action or in quiet stillness, it is the simple, direct emptying of our selves in love and wonder that opens our being to God. Then a day might come when we catch glimpses of God's presence everywhere and in everything. We will have begun to know what it is to pray without ceasing.

This wondering love-longing is a gift from God to begin with, placed deep inside us. We yearn for God because God yearns for God's Self in us and as us. Our part is to bring our small, human will fully to this yearning, to become a profound willingness, a sanctuary where God is returned to God.

We can participate in this not so much by feeling, but by choosing to align ourselves with what God has placed within us. Feelings come and go. We are up one day and down another. The world calls us in so many countless ways, and we cannot help but have feelings about anything and everything. That is not so important. What *is* important is our constancy. Constancy is based on daily choice. No matter how we feel, when we light the wick of our willingness in whatever small means we can hold on to, we begin to open to love. The deepest part of love is ultimately willingness. It is the most precious gift we can return to the Giver of all gifts.

Offering our willingness day after day, moment by moment, in joy and despair, in seeming boredom and intense participation, in resistance and in action, in stillness and exuberance, we will surely be transformed. We will be united not only to our own core but also to Life itself. In time we will experience that we have been, and always will be, held in God's being. Then we might come to feel that we are being prayed. Our journey will no longer be experienced so much as a journey *to* God as a journey *in* God. We will understand that our persons and our lives are fundamentally prayer.

And yet, there is the simple way

to ask each day

for God's way in us.

INVITING SILENCE

"Norris pens an invitation and a challenge: be still. . . . She chooses an evocative form for her words: a kind of spiritual blank verse, short unrhymed lines that themselves encourage slow reading and pausing to think and digest. This book successfully gives a gentle nudge toward a demanding spiritual discipline."

—PUBLISHERS WEEKLY

"Luminous and elegant, it takes us step by step through the process of meditation and answers our most important questions about spiritual practice. It is a jewel of a book."   —GAIL STRAUB

"Norris has always demonstrated a keen sense of everyday spirituality, so it's natural that she would encourage us to find stillness in the midst of our hectic lives. . . . This fine paperback is an invitation to integrate silence into our lives before it becomes an even more endangered resource."   —SPIRITUALITY & HEALTH

JOURNEYING IN PLACE

"With a strong sense of wonder, Norris's shimmering prose commemorates a long-awaited February thaw, the refined blooms on spring's first wildflowers. . . . These considered reflections are imbued with the grace of one who recognizes radiance in the unadorned gifts of a garden's regular cycles of growth and rest."

—BOOKLIST